Competenc Interviewing: The Competitive Advantage

by William Illing

Illustrations by Stephsartwork_

William illing

Acknowledgements

What set out as a personal journey could not have been accomplished without the participation of people who were prepared to take the extraordinary step of sharing their own Competency-Based Interview example answers, which for many of them had been instrumental in securing their next role.

Many of these clients had been made redundant in 2020 during the height of Covid19 market disruptions and they were competing for roles at some of the most desirable companies, at all levels from Analyst to Senior Director, against not just external but internal applicants as well, at a time when there were significantly fewer roles to be found.

Whilst writing this book it occurred to me that even if I succeeded in providing you with a greater understanding of the concepts of CBI and guide you to create stronger examples than you have previously put together, that you would need to be able to compare and contrast your own examples against those who have gone before you, even for roles with organisations who have set the bar the highest, such as with Amazon.com or Google LLC.

I have always been deeply dissatisfied with the examples that are to be found online or on digital media, as they always seem to lack authenticity and specificity, and to be honest, would not meet the rigour that leading companies across all sectors would demand.

I extend my gratitude therefore to Laura, Ian, Christopher, Sanny, Matthew, Kelli, Teresa and the others who have asked for complete anonymity, in their willingness to provide their own material.

I would also like to let the illustrator know just how glad I am that she chose to continue to work on this project with me, despite my many changes of mind on title, design and drawings. Thank you, Stephanie. And finally, to my family, including my mother and my daughter Charlotte and friends, thank you to everyone who has had to tolerant my endless chatter about this project.

William illing

TABLE OF CONTENTS

THE AUTHOR, THE RESEARCH AND THE CREDENTIALS

In effect this book has been in research for the last 25 years, originally stemming from a dissertation written for a Masters, on the most accurate recruitment methodologies to predict success in a role, during which time I first came across the benefits of Competency-Based Interviewing (CBI), followed by two decades of working in talent acquisition, executive search and most recently outplacement, or as it is more commonly known today, career transition.

I've been fortunate enough to lead the recruitment functions of companies such as Microsoft UK and whilst in Consultancy had the opportunity to manage the recruitment operations of businesses drawn from a multitude of sectors such as Retail, FMCG, Software Consultancy and Pharmaceuticals. Within headhunting, I've led assignments to recruit candidates within sectors such as Financial Services, Private Equity and Public Sector.

Having a strong grasp of the behaviours required for someone to succeed in a role and how to utilise CBI to identify the candidates with the requisite behavioural traits led to a greater likelihood of improved decision making in the selection of candidates, their subsequent hiring, and their performance in the role.

Working within Career Transition today, I have between 75-100 clients at any one time, assisting them on a wide range of recruitment and selection methods and which has co-incidentally provided a front-row window seat to the recent growth in demand for Competency-Based Interviews (CBI) in all sectors and at all levels. This has led to an opportunity to build up an understanding of the most common Behavioural Competencies being sought by companies today and which ones are trending up and which ones are trending in the opposite direction.

Since entering Career Transition I've become acutely aware that candidates attending a CBI are still largely unsure as to how they are being evaluated despite literature sent to them by the recruiting company and research they have done independently on the Internet. This led me to write and deliver workshops on CBI, which in turn has given me a wider appreciation of how to coach skills in CBI and handle the many concerns that candidates have with this methodology.

Some of these clients that I have worked with have generously provided their own examples to give you a better appreciation of what a good CBI example answer looks like. During the course of this book, I will refer to CBI, which as you may have already worked out could mean either Competency-Based Interview or Competency-Based Interviewing.

INTRODUCTION & HOW THIS BOOK WILL HELP YOUR CBI SKILLS?

You've probably arrived at this book because you are looking for a new job and want to prepare for a Competency-Based Interview (CBI), either within your current company or with a new employer, or, rather less likely, but no less daunting, your employer could be making redundancies and they could be using CBI to help determine who stays and who goes.

If you are looking for a fulfilling role in a top tier company, in whatever sector, then you are most likely going to be asked to attend a CBI at some point in their recruitment process and you will probably need to provide compelling example answers to their CBI questions, in what will be a competitive market, where the person with the best examples is most likely going to win the role.

If you have bought this book then you are probably like many of those that have attended my workshops previously on CBI, who wish to increase their opportunity to succeed in attaining the right move for them and are prepared to go further than their competition by being far better informed than those that are simply pouring over the internet and finding the same limited information online. That won't be sufficient research for those that want to be more enlightened and desire the advantage gained by understanding what is really going on in a CBI and how to put together excellent example answers that will score maximum points.

Competency-Based Interviewing (CBI) is far more prevalent today than it was when I started utilising CBI some 25 years ago. Whilst I still come across opinions even today that CBI is a fad that will fade, the reality is that it has been on the rise for 25 years, though recently there has been a discernible increment in the last few years, probably as a result of commercial companies adopting similar recruitment methodologies of some of the most successful businesses.

Not only are technology businesses such as Amazon.com and Google LLC requiring a greater focus on CBI to identify talent that can address some of their greatest challenges today, such as; enhanced collaborative activities, internal and external conflict, increased role ambiguity, but so too are non-technology sector businesses within Consumer, Finance Services, Pharmaceuticals, Management Consultancy and Retail also turning to CBI to assist them in finding the right staff with the most desired behavioural competencies. The Public Sector and Not-For-Profit organisations have been consistently utilising CBI to recruit higher calibre staff and to reduce bias.

Whilst there is an increasing number of companies operating Competency-Based Interviews and the demand for candidates to perform at a higher level on these interviews has grown, the quality of information to be found to assist the candidate, whether on the Internet or even emailed to candidates by the company conducting the interview, has remained unevolved and in many cases largely ineffective.

In all the years I have been conducting Competency-Based Interviews, I have been conscious that many candidates struggle with putting together good examples that met or exceeded what was expected of them from their example, but it has only been through coaching these skills to clients who are about to attend a CBI, have I become aware of the disconnect between what is really going on in a CBI and so much of the standard advice given to candidates, most notably that candidates should prepare examples that fit into the framework of STAR (Situation, Task, Action, Result).

It will become abundantly clear to you as you go through this book why this method is focusing your attention in the wrong places and can lead to misinterpretation of what the company is expecting from you and your examples. More on this later, as there is far more to understanding how to do CBI well, than just which behavioural competency framework to use.

It is important to understand the real purpose of CBI as this will form the building blocks of your ability to go on and develop strong examples for CBI. The Chapters on 'What is a CBI' and 'Why is CBI quickly replacing other forms of Interviews' will give you a deep grounding in CBI and prevent you from falling for disinformation on the topic for which there is a considerable amount of, and you may already be under some misunderstandings.

Many candidates view CBI as some 'buzz-word bingo' or 'management speak' exercise and their examples are typically very weak because of this belief, as they miss the point of the exercise. Some candidates attempt their best, but struggle to differentiate between talking about what they specifically did and talking in generalisations, or believing the interviewers are interested in their opinions just as much, if not more than their actions, or not knowing the difference between an experience that happened and some hypothetical activity that only took place in their mind. If you don't think you do any of the above, then you can skip the Chapter on 'Why candidates often struggle with CBI', but you might be deluding yourself, as very few clients I meet for the first time don't make at least one of these mistakes.

In 'How to do CBI well" the competitive advantage will start to separate itself further from any other advice you may have received, as we start to develop your ability to understand the meaning of popular behavioural competencies, widening your appreciation of them, which can be typically quite limited for many candidates who haven't worked within talent acquisition or human resources before.

In 'How to Structure your Examples & Why CAR Over STAR I will demonstrate why CAR (Context, Action, Result) is a far more effective method for formulating your examples than STAR (Situation, Task, Action, Result) and will increase the advantages you have over other candidates, as you will be able to focus your examples on the component parts that score the most points.

Finally, in 'What does Good look like', there is a breakdown for each of the most popular behavioural competencies, the behavioural traits that are most indicative for each competency and examples from clients of mine, ranging from good to excellent, to give you a strong reference point as to what you are trying to build for yourself.

CBI: The Competitive Advantage will give you an understanding of the most popular behavioural competencies sought by companies today, such as:

- Customer Focus
- Collaboration
- Conflict Resolution
- Honesty & Integrity
- Leadership
- Managing Multiple Priorities
- Problem Solving
- Influence & Persuasion
- Challenging the status quo
- Dealing with Ambiguity

Within these chapters, there is specific guidance to:

- *develop your understanding of behavioural competencies*
- *assist you through the development of your own examples to meet the requirements of the behavioural competencies*
- *build an understanding of what to focus on in your examples, enabling you to better align your actions/activities to the behavioural competencies*
- *review examples drawn from Analysts through to Senior Directors, written for interviews with global corporate businesses of all sectors that will enable you to compare and contrast your own examples*

Being able to explain to my clients what is going on in a Competency-Based Interview has been a key differentiator for them and from their feedback, they have attested that without this insight and the step-by-step guide they received, that they would not have performed so well in the CBI. These clients have been extremely generous in contributing example answers that I've put at the back of the book to assist you, many of these examples were instrumental in assisting them in successfully achieving their next role.

The purpose of this book is to provide you with the same competitive advantage that they received, though there are no set magic answers. Your examples must come from your own specific experiences and the interviewer will likely probe into the events you describe in your example, therefore plagiarising other examples that were not your experience are doomed to failure. Instead, if you utilise this guide to develop your understanding of the most popular behavioural competencies sought by organisations today and the step-by-step guide for developing your own examples, which you can review against those provided by my former clients you can be confident that you will be able to develop compelling/winning examples for CBI.

And if you can do CBI well, then you can do any interview well.

WHAT IS A COMPETENCY-BASED INTERVIEW?

Competency-Based Interviewing as it is most commonly known as, Behavioural Based Interviewing which is a better description of the focus of the interview, or as it was originally referred to structured interviewing, is concerned with eliciting examples drawn from your experience, which provide evidence of the range and quality of the behaviours you possess, against the range and quality of the behaviours known to be required for the role.

The questions are designed specifically to encourage you to provide examples from your experience, because if you have performed the desired behavioural competencies in the past then you have the ability to perform them well again in the future. It is allied to the principle that past performance is the best predictor for future performance and is more grounded in behavioural science than it is an HR 'buzz-word bingo' or 'management speak lingo' exercise that many candidates think of it as.

Questions would be phrased like this:
'Can you tell me about a time when you had to handle numerous priorities?'
'Can you give when an example of when you turned around a poor performing team?'
'When have you made a mistake and how did you deal with it?'
In February 2021 there were numerous articles across many media sites about the questions Elon Musk asks candidates to determine if they are good enough to be part of his Space X Project, 3 of which are:

When have you failed and how did you learn from it?
Tell us about a time when you had to solve a problem with little to no information about it.
What kinds of challenges have you faced and how did you overcome them?

As these were questions asked by Elon Musk, the slant of the articles suggested that only a genius like Elon Musk could come up with this line of brilliant questioning. In reality, these types of CBI questions have been asked for a long time and are in common usage today by many organisations, not just at Space X Project. Later, I will look at the behavioural competency Problem Solving and what type of evidence companies are typically expecting candidates to be able to demonstrate in their example to this question.

CBI focuses on how you perform your duties, in essence your behaviours, the combination of the range and quality of behaviours will drive the outcome, which is why the questions focus on encouraging candidates to think about how they perform tasks.

Therefore, CBI is not designed to focus on your:

- *knowledge*
- *experience*
- *learned skills e.g., typing, programming*

Most companies will inform you when you will be coming in for a specific Competency-Based Interview, though some companies will be less structured and will mix in some competency-based questions with other questions designed to focus on some of what is listed above. Either way it pays to be ready for the behavioural based questions.

By deliberately constructing questions that encourage candidates to talk about their specific activities during an event in the past, the interviewers are signalling that they are far more interested in the actions of the candidates that demonstrate the required behaviours, than they are interested in the opinions that the candidates have of their own behaviours. Many candidates unfamiliar with the purpose of a CBI want to express their opinions on their own behaviour through sound-bite type statements, but a CBI is grounded in finding facts that demonstrate the desired behaviours, not in finding opinions.

The behaviours the interviewers are most interested in are the ones that the company has researched and identified are the most important to achieve success within the role, which could also be consistent across the business.

CBI is therefore part Behavioural Science. Companies will conduct research into what behaviours are driving the success of their company e.g., collaboration and also aware of other behaviours that are causing failures e.g., a silo mentality.
Companies performing CBI will dive deeper and define what are the underlining behavioural traits for each behavioural competency. For example, the behavioural competency 'leadership' may mean to one company behavioural traits such as:

- *a leader who wants the very best for their team*
- *someone who takes ownership of the team's self-development and is constantly looking to raise standards*
- *an individual who can make a significant improvement to poor or mediocre performing members of their team*

In another company they might emphasise delivering results above some of the qualities mentioned above.

Virtually every candidate will possess all of the behavioural competencies required by the company, CBI is not a binary exercise as to whether you possess all of them or not, the interviewers are trying to ascertain the range and quality you possess for all of the behavioural traits associated with all of the behavioural competencies for which they are recruiting.

For example, when assessing a candidate's ability to resolve a problem, it is not enough to have an example that is as simplistic as one candidate once replied, 'the customer informed me that there was a problem with their technology and so I ran through a diagnostic check and identified that the customer hadn't plugged in their computer'. A problem has been resolved, but it is of such a low level that it is not demonstrative of problem-solving skills to anything but the most fundamental level, even if that. In this instance, I asked the candidate if they had a better example, one with more complexity.

A candidate's example answers will be evaluated after the interview and graded for the range and quality of the behavioural traits' indicative of the behavioural competency that were notable during the example given by the candidate. Some candidates are confused by the sheer volume of notes being taken during a CBI.

As well as the behavioural science element there is also an element of Art to the process, as although it is only the evidence in the example answer given by the candidate that scores points, at times there may also be the need for interpretation, as to whether an action taken by a candidate is sufficient evidence of the quality of the behaviour required or not, but if two experienced behavioural competency interviewers are evaluating the example answers of a candidate then there should not be much of a disparity in the marking.

The scoring and grading in more detail

I've added this section as I believe that this extra level of detail could be beneficial to you ultimately in fully developing your examples, but if you want to skip forward to the next chapter because you need to prepare for a CBI interview, you can come back to this later.

Let's consider a role for a Secret Agent. Now in terms of knowledge and experience that is indeed a very highly specialised role, but what do you think are the behaviours that are very important for that role?

Probably you would expect to see some behavioural competencies such as Attentive to Detail, Influence and Persuasion, Problem Resolution, Creative Thinking, Copes well under Pressure (not necessarily in that order). Some of these behavioural competencies may be very relevant to the role you do, or want to go on and do, even if it has nothing to do with being a Secret Agent.

In our imagined CBI for recruiting a Secret Agent, candidates would be asked for an example for each of these behavioural competencies. Let's look at one of these, such as 'Copes well under Pressure'. The interviewers would listen to the example given by each candidate for this behavioural competency, and they would ask additional follow-up questions related to the example given.

After the interview with each candidate, the range and quality of the behavioural traits demonstrated within the example given by the candidate associated with 'Coping well under Pressure' could then be identified and plotted against various levels from Level 1 to Level 5 (the highest level) against the pre-determined behavioural traits for the role.

A grading system for the Behavioural Competency 'Copes well under pressure' could be as follows:

Level 5
The example given demonstrated that even under the most intense pressure, the candidate never gave away information, remaining calm, cool, and collected. Able to be logical despite the circumstance and demonstrated that they seized the opportunity to remove themself from the situation they find found themselves in. Was able to report back to base with information gathered at the time to use to defeat the competition comprehensively.
Level 4
The example demonstrated that whilst under intense pressure, the candidate only gave away some information, but none of it was detrimental to our efforts and for most of the time remained calm and composed and smartly took the opportunity to escape when the chance
occurred. Came back with some useful knowledge that enabled us to gain an advantage on the competition
Level 3

The example demonstrated that whilst under intense pressure the candidate was likely to give away information that threatened to expose some of our weaknesses to the competition. Remained calm and collected for about half the time and managed to escape by some good judgment and some luck, though information brought back on the competition was not significant enough to usefully exploit.
Level 2
The example demonstrated that as a secret agent this candidate was likely to give away most of our secrets under scrutiny and likely to panic in an intense situation. Managed to escape, though this was largely due to more luck than judgment and failed to collect any information that was of any significance to our understanding of the competition.
Level 1
The example demonstrated that the candidate had panicked all the way through the interrogation and gave away all our secrets, managing only to return when the captors let the candidate go.

How important the behaviour competency is to the successful performance of the role is the key determining point for companies as to where they will set the Minimum Level Requirement for a pass on each behavioural competency. In our imagined Secret Agent role, the Secret Service might want to set the bar at 5 for all of its behavioural competencies, but then you might find that no one reaches a level 5 on all of the behavioural competencies. You can give half-point grades, where an individual displays a mixture of traits between one level and the next one up. Perhaps you want 4.5 as your Minimum Level Requirement for your Secret Agent on 'Copes well under Pressure and the other behavioural competencies to ensure you still hire the very best, but at least have a reasonable number of Secret Agent.

For an example that is more common to most businesses where an Executive/Personal Assistant is being recruited, a behavioural competency Minimum Level Requirements for this role in a very busy business function might be something like (where 5.0 is the highest level):

Manage multiple priorities -4.5
Responsiveness – 4.5
Discretion -4.0
Honesty & Integrity – 4.0
Conflict Handling- 4.0

Here I have mixed in Behavioural Competencies (Managing Multiple Priorities, Responsiveness, Conflict Handling) and behaviours more associated with Values such as (Discretion, Honesty & Integrity).

Values and how they also factor into CBI

In addition to behavioural competencies, many organisations and public sector bodies will also state their company values and will look to recruit new employees that not only embody the behavioural competencies but also their company values. CBI is also the best interview methodology to measure if a candidate has the desired values to the required level.

Rolls-Royce currently states its values as Trust, Integrity, and Safety. They further define these as being Trusted to deliver excellence, act with Integrity, and operate safely.

They also publish their key behavioural competencies as Agility, Boldness, Collaboration, Simplicity.

Some companies, like Netflix, add behavioural competencies and values together and call them Values. Netflix calls them Real Values and suggests that the more these pertain to you, the more you are likely to enjoy working at Netflix. They are as follows;

JUDGMENT, COMMUNICATION, CURIOSITY, COURAGE, PASSION, SELFLESSNESS, INNOVATION, INCLUSION, INTEGRITY, IMPACT

Why companies choose one candidate over another from a CBI

In companies where they place considerable emphasis on the outcome of the CBI then it is likely that the candidate that grades out the highest will get the role, but other companies may want to balance the CBI with other assessment methods, such as a candidate's cognitive ability, experience, and knowledge relevant to the role. In this situation candidates will normally need to at least pass the minimum level required for each behavioural competency to be seen as a viable candidate before their cognitive ability, experience and knowledge are also taken into consideration.

By the final stage of the recruitment process the remaining candidates should be relatively similar regarding experience, knowledge, skills, but where there will often be significant differentiation between the top 3-5 candidates is in their behavioural competencies. Often one candidate will stand out from the rest in terms of having demonstrated that they were stronger for example in their:

- ability to lead and motivate a team
- collaborate well at all levels
- attention to detail

Candidates succeed at CBI because they are better able to provide specific evidence within their example answers of the behavioural traits indicative of the behavioural competencies that the company is seeking. One major reason why one candidate might succeed over the other candidates is that that candidate possesses the required behavioural competencies at a higher level than the other candidates.

Yet because of the lack of understanding as to the true intentions of a CBI, my experience has shown that there may be many other reasons for one candidate to succeed over another, such as:

- one candidate had a better grasp of the meaning of behavioural competencies required, so could match their examples better to the required behavioural competencies or

- that one candidate better evidenced the required behavioural competencies in their examples than the other candidates, who didn't know how to articulate their examples as well

I hope to level this playing field for you in the pages to come by giving you a greater appreciation not only of what CBI is truly about, but a deeper appreciation of the meaning of the most sought-after behavioural competencies by corporate businesses and public sector organisations today and the tools to be able to build your own examples that meet the required levels of range and quality.

WHY IS CBI QUICKLY REPLACING OTHER INTERVIEW FORMATS?

Better predictor for success

One of the reasons candidates are unprepared for CBI is that they have convinced themselves or been convinced by others to believe that there isn't anything to CBI. Those of us who have used it consistently throughout our careers have witnessed significant value from its usage. Amazon primarily employs CBI techniques to identify their new recruits, and a large meta-analysis conducted in 1998 by Schmidt & Hunter in The Validity and Utility of Selection Methods in Personnel Psychology, demonstrated that structured interviewing techniques (CBI) were far more likely to result in a successful hire than unstructured interviewing.

A recent client informed me that her previous company didn't do CBI, nor did she believe that she needed to do it to find the right candidates for her team, as she explained, 'I just ask them "how did you handle rejection or a situation of conflict when presenting to the Boardroom" and "when have you made a mistake and how did you deal with it?" She was confident that based on their answers and her instinct that she would know which candidate to choose.

I advised her that these are good questions that are commonly asked in CBI and that all that was missing was for her to question her instinct until she was able to articulate what the actions/responses were that she was looking for from a candidate. When this client departed from her employer, a large clothing retailer, her knowledge of what it took to succeed in the business went with her.

Schmidt & Hunter also found that cognitive ability was also a strong predictor for success in a role. If you look at Google's recruitment process it is a heavy dose of CBI and cognitive ability questions. They are known to ask cognitive ability questions such as 'How many golf balls does it take to fill a 747?' In fact, this question I believe is no longer asked, as too many candidates know about it before they attend the interview. In addition to these 2 main methodologies to predict success, Google also looks at a candidate's relevant experience and cultural fit through questions to ascertain if a candidate has the right amount of 'Googleyness".

CBI reduces biases

In addition to being the best predictor of future performance in an interview format, CBI also has the benefit of reducing the potential for biases to creep into an interview process unconsciously.

Before an interview can take place a company/organisation should have undergone a thorough process to determine what behaviours are required to perform well in the role. Once all interested parties (Leaders, HR, peers, employees that report into the role) have contributed to the development of understanding, each person conducting the CBI should be given:

- *A pre-determined standardised set of CBI questions*
- *an understanding of what kind of evidence given by the candidates in their example answers would be indicative of the behavioural traits being sought*
- *a table (See table for Copes well under pressure- Secret Agent) against which it will be possible to plot the candidate's range and quality of actions notable from their examples*

The purpose of the interviewer is to collect all the evidence of the behaviours the candidates have demonstrated in their example answers and grade them accordingly. Although there could be small variances between interviewers on exactly where to grade a candidate, the interviewers have the opportunity to discuss the evidence afterwards and decide on an agreed grade based on the evidence within the example. This should reduce the chances of variability and unconscious bias more than in interviews where the decision-makers are relying on less structured interview methods.

It is worthwhile for anyone conducting interviews, no matter how confident you are in your ability to conduct interviews without bias, to take the implicit bias test run by Harvard University.

Even when using CBI, it is still good practice for interviewers to have a more complete understanding of what unconscious biases they may have and how this could influence their decision-making.

To hire the best people, without fear of bias, it is critical that any company taking Diversity & Inclusion seriously is conscious of how their current recruitment practices impact the success of their D&I goals. CBI implemented, coached, and executed well will identify the best candidates for hire better than any other method of interviewing.

Cost reduction

Recruitment, with or without recruitment agencies fees, can be an expensive activity for any business. To reduce costs, it is better to get it right the first time and CBI methodology can assist in the reduction of recruitment costs because:

- *candidates that better match all the behavioural competencies are not only likely to perform better in the role they are also more likely to stay longer*
- *these candidates are more likely to be promoted*
- *these candidates could transfer more easily into different roles*
- *the cost of replacing a poor hire is felt in terms of additional time spent on finding a replacement as well as additional recruitment fees*

Now that you are aware of why it is popular and why it will remain so, let's get to work on improving your CBI skills.

WHY YOU MIGHT STRUGGLE WITH CBI AT FIRST?

No matter how clear you are with some candidates that you want them to provide a specific example drawn from their experience when answering a CBI question, many candidates will often find it easier to talk about what they believe they would 'normally' or 'usually' do, or they will talk you through a hypothetical situation or provide a range of opinions on how good they would be in a situation related to the question.

But these are the type of statements that anyone could make, they are not grounded in facts, there is no evidence. Whilst the candidate might be convinced that they would do those things, in a CBI the Interviewers are almost solely concerned with facts, anything else is just the creation of an illusion. These kinds of answers may sound fine in other forms of interviews, but CBI is about making decisions on candidates based on the factual evidence gathered, it is not about offering the role to the best illusionist.

Avoiding the bumps in the road

Let's try to prevent you from falling into these common pitfalls candidates of all levels put themselves in and eradicate them from your examples.

Generalisations

In a CBI you might be asked a question like, 'Can you give me an example of a project which required considerable leadership skills?'

To which you might get this response:

'Well, I identify what the business goals are and which ones are the responsibility of my team and divide the duties up based on the skill-set of my team and what I feel would motivate them to do well. Normally, I keep track of their performance, monitoring activities and energy levels, and motivate or push dependent on what I believe will lead to the best outcome'.

This might seem like a reasonable example, but it has failed to pass the test of being an example drawn from a specific event, instead, this candidate has made a statement of how they believe they 'normally' or 'generally' lead a team. The Interviewers should encourage this candidate to talk about a specific project or a time when they led like this so that the Interviewer can find specific instances of the behavioural traits that they are looking for, but if this candidate sticks to only sound-bite type statements that lack detail, then few, if any points can be awarded.
I've began working with clients that have given these types of answers previously and believed that had delivered a good example, only to have become confused when they were informed that they were no longer being considered for the role.

Later we will investigate what makes for good leadership, but for the purpose of this section, I only want you to realise that answers that talk in generalisations and that lack detail are not going to score and grade out well in a CBI.

Hypothetical Answers

In a CBI you may get a question like: 'Can you give me an example of a project you were working on where there was pressure to get it delivered on time?'. To which there are often responses similar to this:

'Well, in that situation I would make a plan of everything that needed to be done and then I would keep a track of all the activities in a spreadsheet and I would make sure that my stakeholders were kept up-to-date with the progress, and I would make sure everything was delivered on time'.

Again, it isn't a real example, it is just a hypothetical answer, what the candidate believes they would do, rather than an example drawn from their experience. The use of the conditional term 'would', confirms to the interviewer that the candidate is not speaking about a real event, it is at best their interpretation of what they think they should do to ensure they deliver their projects on time. It may be that the candidate does do this all the time, but equally, it may be that the candidate has never operated in this way, but the interviewer hasn't been able to gather any definitive evidence and so won't be able to find behaviours indicative for this behavioural competency.

Hopefully in this situation, the interviewer would remind the candidate that the examples need to be from a specific event and would allow the candidate to recall another example drawn from a specific event, though the chances are that if the candidate is having to recall an example on the spot, it is unlikely to be as good as the one that they could have prepared.

In a non-CBI interview, it is possible that you could be asked a question that starts 'what would you do if.....? Now, this is a deliberate hypothetical question, but it is not a CBI question and shouldn't be asked in a CBI interview. I'm not going to go into detail about the best way to answer questions that are not CBI questions, but suffice to say that in this circumstance you would answer a hypothetical question with a hypothetical answer.

Opinion Based Answers

In a CBI you could get a question like:

"Tell me about your last role, how did you build rapport with your team? To which you would often hear a response like this:
Well, I'm a very driven person, I focus on what needs to be done and I just get on and do it well. I work well with other people and can also work well on my own. My colleagues tell me that they like working with me and they like the fact that I am honest and hardworking. I'm good at solving business problems and I am comfortable with working with people at all levels of the organization.

I'm sure you have spotted that this is just their own opinion of themself and not an example drawn from a specific event.

I've come across plenty of candidates who believe that the CBI will be easy because all they will need to do is regurgitate the behavioural competencies as though they are some form of 'management speak' and the more times they use words like 'collaboration' or 'comfortable with ambiguity' they are likely to do well. It doesn't matter how often you use the words associated with the behavioural competencies that matter, it is the quality and quantity of your Actions within your specific examples that provide the evidence of the required behaviours, that is what matters because that is what scores the points that enable you to grade out well to meet or exceed the minimum level required.

Hypothetical, generalised, or opinion-based answers will score 0 points.

Look at this detailed response to a CBI question posed to a client of mine for them to submit online, which was their answer to the question; 'can you provide an example of your leadership and communication style'.

I am a collaborative transformational leader. I build relationships with my team and cross-functional teams by encouraging, inspiring, and motivating them; getting to know them at the start I understand what motivates them - intrinsic and/or extrinsic and I cater my approach specifically to the individual. We say there is no I in team but there are many "I"s .. Each person is a unique individual and needs to be treated as such to make the team stronger.

I look to help bridge the gap between their role and the overall KPIs/Goals - how it ladders up. I have an open-door policy and consider myself a part of the team.
My communication style is assertive. I am very direct, transparent - communicate openly and often, however, I understand the importance of tailoring my communication style to others/my audience. My employees, cross-functional teams, and stakeholders. Understanding each person's style helps me to better relate, motivate and encourage them to fulfil their role.

This answer looks detailed on their leadership and communication style, but it is just lots of opinion-based statements, it is not an example drawn from a specific event where their behaviours are evidenced by their actions. Fortunately, we were able to discuss this example before it was submitted.

HOW TO DO COMPETENCY BASED INTERVIEWS WELL

Basic Maintenance of your CAR

Before uncovering some of the secrets to doing CBI well and giving you the competitive advantage you are seeking, there are some universal best practices to all interviewing skills, including CBI, such as;

- dress appropriately for the interview
- research the company
- research the people you will be meeting
- understand how you meet the job description in terms of the skills, experience, knowledge as well as the behavioural competencies and values
- Have examples prepared for all the above
- Be respectful to everyone you meet
- Give yourself the time you need to answer the question, don't rush
- Try to relax and enjoy the experience
- Arrive a little early, whether face to face or by Video Conference
- Have prepared some questions for the interviewer, the responses to which will help you decide whether you will want the role
- Look to build rapport, but don't be concerned when you meet someone who doesn't want to reciprocate
- Understand what the remaining process will be

Charging your CAR

Make sure you have a good understanding of the full meaning of each of the behavioural competencies for which you will be interviewed.

One significant competitive advantage that you can give yourself ahead of the competition is to delve deeper into the behavioural competencies. Most candidates jump to a quick assumption on the meaning a behavioural competency, forming a very limited perspective, without taking the time to try and understand more of the behavioural traits that are associated with each of the behavioural competencies.

Look at these behavioural competencies from a global pharmaceutical company, taken from their information pack given to candidates ahead of a CBI interview:

· Problem-solving
· Leadership
· Customer Service

We've learnt that this pharmaceutical company are looking for someone good at Problem Solving, but what do you think being good at Problem Solving is all about? What traits would you expect someone to demonstrate in their examples if they were a good leader? And what are the behaviours associated with someone excellent at Customer Service?

These are questions that you should ask yourself and come up with answers to before attempting to recall a suitable event so that you understand what actions you will want to have demonstrated in your examples. There are Chapters on each of these behavioural competencies later in the book with detailed descriptions of the indictive behavioural traits associated with them.

Whilst most companies give candidates a list of their key behavioural competencies without any deeper insight ahead of the interview, some businesses will give you a wider appreciation of what these behavioural competencies mean to their company in more detail.

Each of Amazon's Leadership Principles (Behavioural Competencies) have both a headline title and deeper insight into their meaning. As Amazon have their own language around behavioural competencies, I've added in brackets how these behavioural competencies are more commonly expressed by other companies. Here are a few of them:

CUSTOMER OBSESSION (CUSTOMER FOCUS)
Leaders start with the customer and work backwards. They work vigorously to earn and keep customer trust. Although leaders pay attention to competitors, they obsess over customers.

HIRE AND DEVELOP THE BEST (LEADERSHIP)
Leaders raise the performance bar with every hire and promotion. They recognize exceptional talent, and willingly move them throughout the organization. Leaders develop leaders and take seriously their role in coaching others. We work on behalf of our people to invent mechanisms for development like Career Choice.

INSIST ON THE HIGHEST STANDARDS (ALSO LEADERSHIP)
Leaders have relentlessly high standards – many people may think these standards are unreasonably high. Leaders are continually raising the bar and drive their teams to deliver high-quality products, services, and processes. Leaders ensure that defects do not get sent down the line and that problems are fixed so they stay fixed.

EARN TRUST (COLLABORATIVE)

Leaders listen attentively, speak candidly, and treat others respectfully. They are vocally self-critical, even when doing so is awkward or embarrassing. Leaders do not believe their or their team's body odour smells of perfume. They benchmark themselves and their teams against the best.

HAVE BACKBONE; DISAGREE AND COMMIT (CONFLICT RESOLUTION)

Leaders are obligated to respectfully challenge decisions when they disagree, even when doing so is uncomfortable or exhausting. Leaders have conviction and are tenacious. They do not compromise for the sake of social cohesion. Once a decision is determined, they commit wholly.

Each behavioural competency/leadership principle is given a wider and deeper meaning by the detail below the headline competency, yet many candidates going on an interview with Amazon often rush to an example that meets their own understanding of the headline title of the behavioural competency, with insufficient consideration to demonstrate in their example the specific actions that they took to meet the extra insight provided.

Amazon will interview every candidate against their behavioural competencies/ leadership principles and every candidate that goes through a recruitment process with Amazon will be asked for examples on all their leadership principles, which is currently 14.

Companies conducting a CBI will have just as much, if not more detail on what each of their behavioural competencies means to them, but unlike Amazon, they, unfortunately, prefer not to share it with candidates.

Companies will have slightly different interpretations on the exact meaning of each of the behavioural competencies that they seek, but many of the key indicative traits for each behavioural competency will be the same or very similar organisation to organisation and I have attempted to detail what I believe most companies are looking for with respect to each of these behaviour competencies and their associated behavioural traits in their respective chapters later in the book.

In workshops I run on Behavioural Competency Interviewing, one of the exercises that would most assist the attendees in developing their grasp of appreciating the meaning attributed to behavioural competencies is an exercise focused on brainstorming a behavioural competency.

On your own or with someone you are with, think of a common behavioural competency such as, 'Collaboration'. When you read the word 'collaboration' what does that mean to you? If you heard that someone you work with is collaborative, what behaviours would you associate with them?

At this stage, you don't need to think of a specific example, only ask yourself the question what is good collaboration? Write thoughts here:

Typically, this would be done within a group scenario, but here you are doing it by yourself or maybe with a partner, so slightly tougher. Here's what I would typically get from a group of delegates:

- *Know who are the people you are collaborating with*
- *Set up regular communication*
- *Communicate well*
- *Listen well and understand opinions/requirements of others*
- *Reach an agreement on what is reasonable*
- *Deliver the project*

How well does your list compare to the list above?

If it does compare favourably then you are on your way to having identified some important behavioural traits associated with 'Collaboration' that could help you to put together a good example.

Within a workshop it is possible to build on these initial findings and as delegates get more confident with their own interpretation of this behavioural competency a much deeper and wider appreciation of this behavioural competency comes into view and by the end of the task the whiteboard on 'collaboration' would look something more like this:

- *Create enthusiasm for collaboration, encouraging others to be more collaborative*
- *Build excellent working relationships*
- *Respectful of everyone you are collaborating with no matter what level and which function*
- *Enjoy working with others who sense this and respond to you favourably*
- *Able to work well with all types of personalities*
- *Have the ability to push back without causing real issues for others*
- *Take more ownership of the end result, even if not in a leadership role*

Probably worth re-iterating that stating these traits in an interview would just be an expression of an opinion, but now that you have an understanding of the wider and deeper meaning of this behavioural competency you can more easily go on to identify the specific event where your Actions are a closer match to the deeper understanding you now have of the behavioural competency.

The process of attempting to think about the wider and deeper meaning of a behavioural competency, plus building an understanding that creates a clearer vision of how previous experiences relate to a behavioural competency can be an 'ah ha' moment for some of workshop delegates. Don't worry if it hasn't been for you, much more insight to come.

HOW TO STRUCTURE YOUR EXAMPLE ANSWERS & WHY CAR OVER STAR

Much of the information to be found on the Internet and even advice that is given by organisations that are delivering CBI has remained the same for decades primarily encouraging candidates to respond to CBI questions by using STAR (Situation, Task, Action, Result). But in CBI or Behavioural Based Interviewing, as it is also called, you can only identify Behaviours from the Actions someone took, you might draw inference from the Result as well, but you certainly cannot spot behaviours from the Situation and the Tasks, as the Situation and the Tasks are just contextual information. Your behaviours are not discernible in the Situation and the Tasks.

Believing the Situation and Tasks to be of significant interest to the interviewer, often leads to candidates spending considerable time preparing and delivering examples with far too much Situation and Task content and far too little detail on the Actions and Results. Whilst the Interviewers are interested in understanding something about the context in which to be able to better judge your Actions and even the Results, they are not awarding points that impact the grading for describing the Situation or the Tasks.

There is also the unintended consequence whereby many candidates assume that in complying with the recommendation to follow the pattern of STAR for each of their examples, that this is of itself what CBI is all about and that therefore they have succeeded in providing a good example purely by following the pattern, even if they have failed to describe a single Action that they took which is indicative of the behavioural competency. This is common when candidates don't appreciate the meaning of a behavioural competency and follow the STAR method slavishly.

This isn't the fault of candidates for this misunderstanding, many companies don't want to share too much insight on the CBI methodology and provide little more insight than STAR, which itself creates a chasm between what the company is expecting the candidate to prepare ahead of a CBI and what the candidate understands they are being asked to provide.

The thought that you have to build your examples using the STAR formula has become a more common misconception recently, probably as a result of both the continuous repetition by companies themselves which has then been picked up ad nauseum online and on digital media, without anyone considering its limitations and unintended consequences.

If you are familiar and comfortable with STAR and want to stick with this method, then I would encourage you to at least not think of STAR as 25/25/25/25% for each part of the formula, and instead think of it more as 10/10/60/20%. Whilst you can flex this guide a little if you need to, it will at least focus your attention where your attention should be, because that is where you can score the points to grade out well.

Even better still by the simple fact that if you call the framework for your example answer CAR (Context, Action, Results), you will be constantly reminded that Context is just Context and that you should focus your attention on your Actions and your Results. More to come on why Actions are especially important.

Ultimately it will be the evidence of your Actions in your example that will decide if you have demonstrated the behavioural competency to the level of quality and range required by the company, more than which formula you use,

CAR or STAR, but the knowledge of where the points are to be found and the understanding of the limited role that the context plays in the evaluation of your example should give you a competitive advantage over other candidates who are spending considerable time finessing their Situation and Tasks for each behavioural competency.

I recommend you use CAR for preparing and delivering your examples answers in all situations, even when the company delivering the CBI has advised you to prepare using STAR as this is will just be guidance, not a directive. The only time I would recommend you stick to STAR is if the role you are going for is one where absolute adherence to procedure far outweighs independent thinking, such as with roles like Air Traffic Controller.

SUPER-CHARGING YOUR C A R

the Context

As already mentioned, the quality of your behaviours will be judged from the evidence provided by your Actions, so the point of the Context is to provide sufficient information for the interviewers, who will also evaluate your examples afterwards, to be able to better appreciate the reasons for the Actions that you took.

The context could be:

- *the company you were working for and the specific role or project*
- *the issues that your company or your role were facing*
- *the Customers/senior management/ vendors requirements*
- *The desired outcome/s sought at the start of the project or your involvement*

Whist many candidates are tempted to want to demonstrate their knowledge and experience during this part of the example, the Interviewers only need sufficient Context to be able to judge your Actions, therefore keep the Context short and what information you do provide, should be congruent with the Actions that you go on to take.

Important notes on the Context part:

- No points are awarded for Context
- Context should be as succinct as possible

- Keep Context relevant to the Actions and Results you are going to go on and describe

Your Actions

Actions are where the vast majority of points are awarded in a CBI and your Actions are concerned with:

- *what you did*
- *why you did it*
- *how you performed the Action (When describing how you performed an activity, you are describing your behaviour)*
- *in some circumstances when you did it (the order of your Actions, may demonstrate logic for problem-solving/decision-making/managing multiple priorities type behavioural competencies)*

Actions are normally expressed through an active verb, for example, 'I identified that there was an issue with the performance of an application and spoke to the software engineering team, who confirmed that this was the case. Afterwards, I met with the Programme Manager who authorised a review and received the sign-off for the required changes.

I oversaw the required improvements to the running of the Application from the software engineering team and monitored the performance of the Application over the next few days and saw no recurrence of the earlier issues.' (Potential example for the Behavioural Competency Problem Solving to demonstrate the active verb).

You are recalling your Actions from a specific event that occurred in the past therefore the active verb will be expressed in the past tense. Here is a list of active verbs that might help you to describe your activities more accurately.

Delivered	Reduced	Corresponded	Composed
Generated	Decreased	Advised	Specified
Expanded	Saved	Discussed	Explained

Gained	Eliminated	Negotiated	Directed
Raised	Consolidated	Wrote	Facilitated
Enhanced	Presented	Persuaded	Guided
Improved	Conveyed	Introduced	Ran
Increased	Addressed	Created	Headed
Oversaw	Shaped	Managed	Anticipated
Forecasted	Championed	Delegated	Motivated
Nurtured	Liaised	Supported	Accomplished
Raised	Transformed	Reformed	Spoke

The quantity and quality of the active verbs you use won't improve your score unless perhaps the behavioural competency is communication skills, but they will assist you in the articulation of your example.

Some candidates appreciate that their Actions are extremely important and make a long list of Actions, but it is the quality of these actions as well as the range of Actions that are indicative of the behavioural traits associated with the behavioural competencies, that are more important than just the number of Actions.

In this example for 'Handling conflict with a customer or customers, there is little in the way of the number of Actions, but there is a high level of quality, 'Our customers were very angry with the level of service they had received and I decided not to say anything at this point, instead I realised that the best thing I could do was to listen to their complaints and let them know that I had heard them and understood their feelings. I was confident that I would win most of them back in time, but today was not the day to talk, it was to be quiet and listen.' In this example, there is very little activity, except listening, but this could be recognised as a strong quality for handling conflict by a company that believed that given the circumstance that this was the right thing to do at the right time.

The Actions you express must be relevant to the behavioural competency for which you have been asked to provide an example. Sometimes candidates express a long list of actions, but very few of these activities pertain to the respective behavioural competency. Actions you took not relevant to the behavioural competency won't score and you probably won't grade out well for that behavioural competency.

For example, this one was given to me by a client of mine, who, having just heard the above points, realised that she had made an error in an example answer she had previously given.

The question posed was 'Can you provide an example of your ability to be innovative?'

Yes, I believe it is important to surround yourself with innovative people, and on a recent project where we needed to launch a new product, I gathered my team around me and we discussed how we could make this product more innovative than the last. I encouraged my team to come up with answers themselves and I took the role of the scribe as we brainstormed how we could come up with something more innovative. I captured and encouraged further suggestions from my team that included aiming at Generation X and to gamify the product more. When we launched the product is was an immediate success.'

As you can see there are numerous actions, but none that would relate to being Innovative, and therefore the Actions don't relate to the behaviour sought in the question. These behaviours could be more easily associated with Leadership traits but would not indicate behaviours associated with being Innovative. This doesn't just happen to this individual; it happens a lot on a CBI.

Asking yourself 'How have I performed these Actions' is probably the most important question you can ask yourself, because when you start exploring 'how' you conducted activities you are articulating your behaviours directly to the Interviewers, rather than requiring them to evaluate your behaviours through a stream of Actions.

For example, on demonstrating Influence & Persuasion skills.

'I had to get approval from the Board of Directors for my idea to open up a new market to launch our range of products. I had researched the new market thoroughly, and in the Board meeting, I presented the Sales and growth forecasts and persuaded them to give me the go-ahead. There was a step before this though, how I got the green light was I contemplated how it would feel if the Board rejected my proposal and what I needed to do to prevent this happening. So first I spoke with the Director of Sales who was impressed with the data supporting the sales and growth forecasts I predicted and he said he would back me in the Board meeting and he informed me that the CEO would be very keen to see the growth forecast, so I spoke with the CEO's EA and got 10 minutes with the CEO the day before the Board Meeting to go over the forecast. The CEO was the first to say in the Board meeting that the research was excellent and very soon every other Board member nodded and gave their approval to launch our products in the new market.'

This example given to me by a client demonstrates not just a list of Actions, but also 'how' they persuaded the Board, in this case primarily through getting advocates with influence over all those involved in the final decision.

When you can see that your Actions directly relate to the behavioural competency in the question, that should indicate to you that you have chosen a good example. If the Actions don't seem to match the behavioural competency, then perhaps you have another example that compliments the behavioural competency better.

As you become increasingly familiar with each of the behavioural competencies you will improve your chances of identifying the right event/experience to match to the behavioural competency.

Resolving the 'I' and 'We' conundrum

Many candidates feel more comfortable saying 'we', even though they mean 'I' in an interview. The Interviewers need to assess what you have done and so if you say 'we' when you mean 'I' they could assume that you are talking about what the team did rather than yourself and there are no points for an activity done by a team. To prevent yourself from saying 'We' when you mean 'I' practice writing down your example answers.

You can always talk about actions that you were involved in with your team or with other leaders, where the term 'we' is more accurate, but after using the term 'we' you should then follow up with the specific action that you took. Such as, "We held a meeting to discuss what we all felt would be the most appropriate action and I decided that I would contact all the customers that had been impacted".

Whilst some clients have expressed concern that they do not want to come across as egotistical by using the pronoun 'I', interviewers are unlikely to find the use of 'I' as evidence of an inflated ego. What would be more concerning around issues of ego would-be candidates repeatedly using adjectives to describe their activities such as, 'I resolved this amazingly difficult business problem and everyone else congratulated me on my brilliance".

Re-capping Actions:

- *The most important aspect of scoring well on a CBI*
- *What, why, how and sometimes when*
- *High quality and range of Actions, trump large number of Actions*
- *Only Actions related to the behavioural competency will score points* • *Know your Active verbs*
- *Your Actions score the points, not the teams or others, so say I, when you mean I*

Your Results

Some companies look at Results as evidence of a behavioural competency others don't and you are very unlikely to know whether they will or will not, but it will help your understanding of CBI to know why some companies don't score for outcomes.

Outcomes are not behaviours, they can on many occasions be impacted by other factors than just your behaviours, for instance by the effort of other individuals, internal company decisions, competition, or lack of it. There is also the issue of the veracity of some candidates, who could exaggerate the outcomes in their examples, and it would be difficult for the interviewers to be able to verify the results.

My instinct is that many organisations, specifically fast-paced companies are likely to want to hear strong outcomes and so it is safer to include examples with positive results. Good outcomes, in my experience, can influence how favourably some interviewers evaluate a candidate's actions, even if they don't specifically grade the result.

In an interview you may be trying to decide between two potential examples, one where your actions are more demonstrative of the behavioural traits associated with the behavioural competency and another where they were less demonstrative of the behavioural competency, but the outcome was better. In this situation I would advise you to use the example where your actions were most demonstrative of the required behavioural competency, but if you want to play it safe, you can also inform them that you also have another example where the outcomes were even better.

Results that are quantifiable, such as new business won, procedures improved or money saved on a project are easier for an interviewer to evaluate and award points for if they are awarding points for the result, than for instance a qualitative outcome such as good feedback, but that doesn't mean you shouldn't include qualitative information.

Your outcomes should be the natural consequence of the specific actions that you took, there shouldn't be an unexpected jump to get from your actions to the result. Such as, 'I spoke to a few customers, and this led to a 100% increase in items sold'.

Some candidates, especially individuals that are very outcome-orientated are prone to focusing too much on the Result. If, this is true of you, then take a moment to realise that it is your actions that lead to the results, not the results themselves that is the focus of the evaluation of your example.

Once you have written out all the outcomes related to your example, check back to the Context and ask yourself are the Context, Actions and Results all aligned.

Summary of Results:

- *Results may or may not be scored, but you can at least influence the score for your Actions with good outcomes*
- *Results should be a natural consequence of your Actions*
- *Fast-paced companies probably want to hear strong results*
- *High-quality and range of actions with low level results should be scored better than poor quality and range of actions, but better outcomes*
- *Your example answers should flow from Context to Action to Result.*

How Long should your CAR example be?

One of the most common questions I get asked is 'how long should my example be?'

There are no time limits given to examples and I can't answer this question in terms of minutes and seconds. The best way I can answer this question is to advise that the length of time should be no longer than the time it takes to include a range of high-quality Actions that pertain to the behavioural competency, plus a succinct Context and Result.

Another way to look at this is, if you feel your example answer is rather short, then there is the potential that you haven't included enough Actions that demonstrate sufficient relevant behaviours to pass the required score to grade out well.

If you feel your example is on the long side, then you should ask yourself is this because I have spent too long focusing on the Situations and Tasks. The Context and the Results should be succinct. If you feel your example is still too long, then review all your Actions and remove ones that aren't related to the behavioural competency.

As your competence in CBI grows, so you will find it easier to know when you have delivered an excellent example, but in the meantime, if you are on a CBI interview and you are unsure as to whether an example has covered sufficient Actions, then you can always ask the interviewer if they are satisfied with your example or if they would like more detail.

Content is King

The Interviewers are focused almost entirely on the content of your examples, specifically the quality and quantity of your Actions as they pertain to the behaviours, that is why you may witness an interviewer making copious notes to evaluate your example answers afterwards. With Video Conferencing it is possible to record the interview. Whilst body language and tone add to the understanding you gain of each candidate, the focus remains on the quality of the content of the example answers.

I've found that once clients start building stronger example answers that provide better evidence of the behaviours, then their confidence grows, and with it comes some incremental improvements in their body language and tone. Therefore, I advise focusing on improving the content of your example answers and improved body language and tone will follow naturally.

It is rare for a candidate to try to lie or embellish the truth in a CBI interview and if they do, they are very unlikely to be able to get into the level of the detail that the Interviewer will want to explore with them, not to catch them out, but in trying to explore their Actions deeper to get to the required behaviours. The incongruency of content, tone and body language will be too obvious, therefore the Interviewer can focus almost entirely on content.

WHAT DOES GOOD LOOK LIKE?

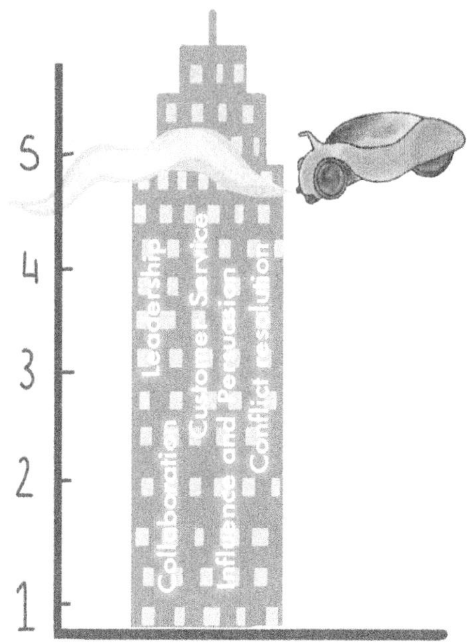

In this chapter, we are going to put it all together with a breakdown of the traits associated with each behavioural competency, through to examples given by clients of mine that have helped them to secure roles in some of the most popular corporations of today. This will lead you to put together your own high flying CAR examples.

In this chapter there is/are:

- *insight on each of the most commonly sought behavioural competencies*
- *some typical questions*
- *an opportunity for you to put together your first draft of your example*
- *some full example answers from clients that they used on their CBI*
- *an analysis of each example answer from an evaluators perspective*
- *a CAR framework for you to develop your own examples*

COLLABORATION

This seems to be the most sought-after Behavioural Competency at the moment. Very few clients go through a recruitment process and not get asked this question.

Questions could be for example:
Tell me about a time when you needed to collaborate with others? When have you collaborated well on a project?

Interviewers know that candidates feel more comfortable answering questions related to their experience more than answering the type of behavioural competency questions as listed above, so an interviewer might look at your CV and ask a question such as "I see on your CV that you worked on an assignment to XXX which would have required a considerable amount of collaboration across the business, tell me how you ensured that the collaboration went well?'

As shown earlier, behavioural traits associated with Collaboration

- *Listening and understanding the thoughts of others*
- *Create enthusiasm for collaboration, encourage others to be more collaborative*
- *Build excellent working relationships*
- *Respectful of all you are collaborating with no matter what level and which function*
- *Enjoy working with others and others sense this and respond to you, favourably*
- *Able to work well with all types of personalities*
- *Have the ability to push back without causing real issues for others*
- *Take more ownership of the end result even if not in a leadership role*

Before looking at some examples from my clients, take some time to think about a specific example from your experience? Opportunity to make some notes here and then build out your example after reading the examples from my clients.

Context

Action (what, why, how)

Result

In laying this out in this format, this should further guide as to where to focus your attention when completing your answer. An Excel spreadsheet is also a common tool for constructing example answers and you may prefer to use Excel, just ensure that the information you put into your Actions column is disproportionately more than for Context and Result.

With the example answers from my clients, please bear in mind that these examples are to help you in your understanding and to inspire you to recall your own examples which you can compare and contrast with your own. They shouldn't be copied in any way, as your example answers need to come from your unique experiences.

Example 1 for Collaboration

Context

Following a restructure, the training department was disbanded and training responsibilities fell to the Medical Science Liaison (MSLs) which resulted in training focusing mostly on clinical papers and was almost entirely PowerPoint driven with limited attention on key selling messages. The impact of which was that the sales team lacked direction on the completion of training. MSLs were protective of their remit and Brand Managers not engaged as do not have a training background.

Actions

I encouraged a more collaborative effort on training and discussed the potential benefit of higher sales performance with MSL and Brand Managers and how this could lighten the load on MSL. Gained support to offer a medical oversight on training materials and also to develop training in a number of areas, including collaborating with experts who could add further insight into our business, patients, and clinicians.

I re-wrote the sales role-play validation training material and then on the training course worked closely with the MSLs. I presented at the start of each training course, to set the scene, led some sessions, and then completed the course with a full day of practice to embed the learning.

Result

This led to an immediate improvement in sales performance.

Analysis

I won't score or grade these examples as there hasn't been the opportunity to probe further which you would have in an interview to get more detail from the candidate.

In this example there is clear evidence of being both collaborative and encouraging greater collaboration between functions demonstrating quality and range of Actions relevant to the behavioural competency. I would want more detail of collaborative activities with Brand Managers and additional experts to probe to see if the candidate can give more evidence of good collaboration skills. Better still not to rely on the Interviewer to ask the right questions and to have a few more collaborative activities.

Example 2 for Collaboration

Context

My team's engagement score was higher than other divisions. Every year the company asked its employees to complete an employee engagement survey which was reviewed at a VP level, the result for my team was consistently 5 to 10 points about average and often 15 to 30 points above the lowest business area. In a conversation with the VP, we agreed that I try to support the other areas to improve their employee engagement score.

Actions

I arranged to discuss with each of the business and functional area heads and listen to their thoughts and ideas. The feedback confirmed that many of their employees felt they were not being challenged and lacked career development coaching and that some of the leadership team also lacked the ability to effectively hold employee development conversations.

I had been a strong proponent of ensuring everybody within my team had an individual development plan (IDP). Having an IDP conversation enabled the opportunity to talk about a person's aspirations and goals over a 5, 10, or even a 15-year period. Discussed the situation with the VP and got his buy-in to create a project with the leadership team and support of a central talent and development resource.

I presented options to the Leadership Team. Some had alternative ideas and I incorporated some of these ideas, e.g. to ensure the program covered key languages and the time that this programme was going to take from their team's resources. I found a workable consensus amongst the leadership and the LT agreed to the plan.

Following continual dialogue with the leadership team, more of them engaged with the programme, and surprisingly 2 of the least enthusiastic members of the LT originally embraced the 'strengths approach' which gave them the confidence and framework to have conversations with their team members. The conversations moved from being solely goal orientated to person orientated.

Result

There were many outcomes. One group radically re-organised. Mainly the result was the ability to talk in a common language about a topic that some people find difficult to talk about. There were more role changes. There was a four-point increase in the career and growth section of the employee survey the following year.

Analysis

There is plenty of evidence of collaboration, including listening and incorporating other ideas into his original plans and gaining trust and credibility as the process went along, despite initial resistance. Originally this example contained more information on talent development and was unnecessarily long, whilst this version has plenty of evidence of the behavioural competency of Collaboration, without needing to go into detail that wasn't relevant to the sought-after behavioural traits.

Your own example for Collaboration

Context

Action (What, Why, How)

Result

CUSTOMER SERVICE

Or Customer Focus or Customer Obsession

A CBI question for Customer Service could be something similar to:
'Can you provide an example of when you gave excellent Customer Service?' or *'Tell me about a time when you went above and beyond to demonstrate your Customer Focus'*

Behavioural traits associated with Excellent Customer Service:

- *Listening and understanding (some traits overlap with others)*
- *Responsiveness and attentiveness*
- *Balancing customer requests and commercial acumen*
- *Building a relationship that will inspire customers to return*
- *Meeting and/or exceeding expectations*
- *Developing credibility and Trust with customers*

Opportunity to make some notes for your own example:

Context

Action (what, why, how)

Result

Example 1 Customer Service | Customer Obsession
Given to a Public Sector organisation

Context
A customer of our branch in Derby had been sent a cheque by our department as re-imbursement for PPI, however, he no longer had a bank account. He had previously had a joint account with his wife, however, he now had advanced dementia and they had agreed to remove his name from the account, so that he wasn't able to access funds without her authorisation. Unfortunately, they had done this instead of applying for power of attorney, so from a legal perspective, it was difficult to prove that she had the right to accept funds intended for him.

Action *I immediately requested for the cheque made out in the customer's name to be stopped, as there was no way it could be cashed and sorting this step first would avoid delays later. I then liaised with our process manager, and the manager of the payments team to discuss ways forward.*

I also kept in regular contact with the manager of the Derby branch to ask what information and evidence the customer was able to provide. After exhausting all of our usual methods of proof, we found that the Department for Work and Pensions were paying our customer's disability benefit payments into his wife's account.
We found this acceptable proof that she had responsibility for his care and also decided that if the government was satisfied, then so were we.

Accepting this also meant that we didn't need to inconvenience the customer further by requesting documentation from them, we could request the payment details from Derby.

I was then able to speak to colleagues I had an existing relationship with on relevant teams to fast-track the payment through and get it paid directly into that account.

Result *I received a commendation from the manager at Derby for the excellent service provided.*

Analysis

Due to the complexity the context is longer than average, but most importantly there is plenty of evidence of the behaviours a company would look for when assessing Customer Service behavioural traits. This client is very comfortable in being specific about what action he took and what actions were in conjunction with other stakeholders involved. He also is very clear with what was an 'I' and a 'We' activity.

Customer Service Example 2

This example was prepared by a client for a giant corporate technology business that looks for candidates who are highly customer focus orientated. Here my client has provided just the notes they made ahead of her CBI meeting, but there is more than sufficient detail to assist you.

Context

Negotiations for the largest partnership for my marketing program > XX hotels (name of hotel chain with-held for reasons of anonymity). They had issues with the clauses of the contract: a) criminal convictions clause b) natural disaster clause

Actions

Managed the communication between them and our legal team with close follow-ups.
From increased communication - learnt that they tended to face onboarding problems with revenue managers. Initiated an onboarding webinar & customized contract to their most important needs.
Through continued follow-ups, they were complimentary of my willingness to listen and champion their needs within my employer and showing initiative to solve problems with them

Result

They added 2 more hotels to the programme because they trusted me to ensure that the programme worked for them

Analysis

Whilst it's a short example, there is some good evidence here of strong customer service in how the candidate is responding to the client and gaining support internally to meet her client's needs. An interviewer should probe deeper to look for more customer service skills within this example and also ask for another example. A candidate strong on customer service should be able to have more than one example.

Your Example for Customer Service

Context

Actions (What, Why, How)

Results

CONFLICT RESOLUTION | EMOTIONAL INTELLIGENCE

Another behavioural competency that is widely sought is the ability to handle conflict.

Typical questions might be:
'Can you describe a time when you had difficulties with a boss/ a key stakeholder/ Customer' (dependent on job role) or 'can you talk me through a conflict you had a work?'

First let's try to understand why the ability to handle conflict is such a popular behavioural competency.

All organisations accept that conflicts can arise and whilst someone could be extremely good at their job, they may tend to either run from all or most confrontations even when absolutely necessary to fulfil key activities within their role or on the other hand, they may become easily annoyed and damage relationships with stakeholders and/or customers.

Most companies seek someone who is good at handling conflict, not just to find someone who can find a resolution, after all that is what the problem resolution question is for, but more importantly to gauge a candidate's Emotional Intelligence (EQ). Can an individual navigate through such stormy waters as for example, resistance, pressure, blame, calmly and professionally until they find a resolution or does an individual lose their self-control quickly and easily?

It's important therefore to talk about the conflict, what was said and how you re-acted through this period. If your example reads more like a business problem resolution, then it's likely that you haven't focused enough on the conflict. Many candidates feel uncomfortable talking about conflict in an interview and stick to just the resolution, but interviewers are likely to be more impressed where a candidate can describe how they handled the conflict, where the tougher the conflict the more likely you will score well, provided off course that you responded well to the conflict.

Many candidates find it easier to give an example where they recall a time when they stepped in between two colleagues or more quarrelling, but in this situation, you are unlikely to be as tested emotionally, so an interviewer is unlikely to get a good sense of your emotional Intelligence from this type of answer.

Any conflict that has been going on for a while and requires a range of emotional intelligence responses is likely to score better than a one-off argument.

Behavioural traits for Handling Conflict:

- *Understanding how the conflict arose*
- *Calmness & Professionalism*
- *Listening well to those with whom you are in conflict*
- *Resilience – the conflict probably didn't go away immediately*
- *Seek to resolve problem despite the level of conflict*
- *Maintain vigour and keep working towards a solution*
- *Influencing skills*

Opportunity to make notes for your own example, ahead of reading the examples made by my clients.

Context

Action (what, why, how)

Result

Example Answer 1 Conflict Resolution

Context

During an Area Sales Manager's meeting, we discussed the agenda for the upcoming Christmas divisional meeting, which would be the first one since the merger and an opportunity to show the sales teams that we were operating on a 'one team' philosophy.

I volunteered to put together a presentation and all Area Sales Managers agreed and once it was in draft form I circulated it, asking for feedback and all feedback was positive.

Action

3 days before the meeting, one ASM sent an email saying that she didn't agree with the idea of a presentation and didn't want their team to take part. I called the Manager, and she was unwilling to go further into her reasons, so I informed her of all the work that had gone into putting it together, the importance of a 'one team' philosophy, the fact that flights and hotel rooms had been booked and that she had initially agreed to this idea. Gained agreement to meet for a one-to-one at Head Office.

At the meeting, I asked the Area Sales Manager how I could regain her involvement. She told me that she would feel undermined if another Manager presented to her team. I apologised to her and informed her that this was not the intention, and that the presentation would be done by all 3 managers, that was always the plan and that she would be able to choose any of the topics and present to all teams, not just her own. We were able to establish that there had been a misunderstanding and that she had been concerned that I was trying to take over her team.

Result

In light of this, the Area Sales Manager re-read the email and realised the true intention of the dynamics of the presentation.

Analysis
The behaviours here are worth noting: not many actions, but there are some high-quality actions such as he handles the conflict well by being both understanding of the sensitivities of his colleague and yet finding ways to move forward, until such time as the colleague has realised the true intention of his actions.

Example Answer 2 Conflict Resolution

When have you had to deal with a difficult stakeholder? (Common conflict handling question)

Context
As part of an evolving Change Management process in a smaller organisation, I was given the task to ensure that all change initiatives were released safely into the live environment Previously there had been little control around the timing of deliveries and any inter-dependencies / threats that clashing implementation dates could cause. I was asked to manage a weekly Change Approval Board (CAB) to conduct this

Action
The IT change was represented by a manager who felt that these changes were unnecessary. I was less senior than this stakeholder and he made me feel uncomfortable by putting down my checks. He was unable to answer questions around the implementation and back-out approaches which meant that I had to request further clarifications before a number of his changes could be approved. He then became aggressive towards me, creating a bad atmosphere within the office

I identified the key criteria that I was looking to solve each week and why I wanted to clarify these. I used these to provide him with the standard questions that I would typically always ask so that there were no surprises
I booked an early morning conversation to step through these with him and said that if those answers were in place, approvals would be easier.

He then built this into his pre-meeting checks with his own IT colleagues so had more information to hand at follow-up meetings which meant that change approval became much quicker without follow-up clarifications needed.

Result

Our relationship improved and he was able to appreciate why the checks were important. He also was able to better plan his own IT changes with inputs from the forum on other critical non-business change that was taking place

My Analysis

Plenty of clear Actions and the candidate has shown a good degree of calmness and the ability to provide a solution, despite what sounds like a very demanding stakeholder. It would be better not to describe/label the stakeholder as being aggressive and just say what he did and let the Interviewers come to the conclusion themselves of his aggressiveness.

Example Answer 3 Conflict Resolution

Context:

In my position as global director, and having recently assumed responsibility for Europe, having been heading up US operations, I had the task of unpicking a number of conflicts within my team and with European customers. The root cause was due to the outgoing GM having lost customer focus and too much negative energy being inwardly targeted.

Action:

There were two courses of action that needed to be taken. Firstly, to engage with our customers. Listen to their concerns and start developing plans to address them. Specifically, the customer was unhappy with the performance of a number of my team members. In the case of an account manager, she needed to be removed from being customer-facing until trust could be rebuilt. Hence, I had her focus more on the behind-the-scenes process and planning. In the case of a couple of engineers, I needed to coach them to become more confident in responding directly to the needs of the customer without being so reliant on running everything through our headquarters in Japan. This engaged the engineers and provided quicker customer service. Additionally, my team seeing me get in front of customers, listening and responding, and taking ownership day to day it focused the team more on the customers and less on each other.

Result:

I would say about 80% of the problems were resolved with these actions. However, there were some issues between certain individuals in the team. In one example I stepped in to support senior management in goal setting and frame working expectations towards their team which after a performance cycle of about a year or so taking place yielded more positive results. In the case of one senior manager responsible for program management, who had been hired before my tenure. He, unfortunately, did not respond to my level of expectations and we had to part company.

Analysis

There is evidence of listening and understanding the concern of the customer and making significant changes to address the conflict with them. Some of the changes made would probably have caused additional conflict internally and these conflicts are not fully addressed in the answer. An Interviewer should look to probe this area further, but even better if the candidate is prepared to provide deeper insight on the conflict, as the heavier and more complex the conflict is, the more points could be scored for handling that conflict well.

Your Example for Conflict Resolution

Context

Action (what, why, how)

Results

Note any opinions or labels you have expressed which are potentially negative e.g. (difficult individual, stressful, argumentative) and remove them. It is better just to describe the events and how you handed the conflict and let the interviewer form their own opinion of the situation and/or the other individuals involved.

HONESTY & INTEGRITY

This behavioural competency or a value is commonly sought through such questions as:

'When have you made a mistake and how did you deal with it?'

'When did you do the right thing?'

Behavioural traits associated with Honesty & Integrity:

- *Have the courage to open up about a mistake immediately*
- *Apologise where necessary*
- *Correct the issue if you can, not afraid to ask for help if required*
- *Identify why you made the mistake*
- *Appreciate what you have learnt from this event*
- *Communicate what actions you take to prevent it from re-occurring*

A behavioural competency question such as this is far more likely to give you a true insight into a candidate's self-awareness and honesty, than the former standard interview questions such as 'what are your strengths?' and 'what are your weakness?', which have virtually disappeared over the last couple of years.

Before reading examples from my clients, what example comes to mind for you?

Context

Action (what, why, how)

Result

Example 1 – Honesty & Integrity

When did you make a mistake and how did you deal with it?

Context

As part of an assignment to oversee the safe delivery of Change initiatives, I was asked early in my career as an Analyst to present a summary of all upcoming releases to the Chief Operating Officer prior to giving final approval. The COO had a formidable reputation and was known to express his views very candidly.

Action

I recognised that I needed to communicate in a clear and concise way to ensure that he understood the deliverables.

I produced a summary one-pager which I felt gave a really clear view of what was being delivered when the systems would have an outage and what the benefits of the delivery would be. I presented these in a clear top-down way where I thought I had got the key points across well, but I made a mistake.

Whilst the info that I had presented was clear, correct, and concise, it had not been the information that the COO had wanted. I had failed to validate and understand his stakeholder needs.

Result

He shared with me that his key concern was about whether any backout plan had been produced, tested, and timed. This was to address his priority to keep live services running.

The learning for me was a reminder to always consider stakeholder perspectives and to ask if unsure rather than assume what a stakeholder may want.

Analysis

In this rather short answer, we still have some quality key behaviours for this competency, namely: an ability to identify a mistake made and to be honest about it. An ability to take the criticism from a senior leader well, note that he doesn't make excuses for his mistake, which hints towards maturity and emotional intelligence and also, he shares what he learnt from the experience, which is important for this behavioural competency.

Example 2 – Honesty & Integrity

When have you made a mistake and how did you deal with it?

Context

I try not to look at mistakes as a failure but as an opportunity for growth, however, as a manager, I also feel it is very important to take personal accountability. Sets the standard for the team.

For example, recently I asked the social team to work with a freelancer to cut a quick turnaround promo as our creative team was slammed (very busy). However, I didn't tell the creative team we were doing this until I shared the promo for their review. As you can imagine, this created a bit of angst with the team leading to the producer attacking our lack of following process in an email directed at me.

Actions

I immediately called the producer and talked her through why we did what we did – I wasn't going around them, I was trying to help them by not adding another project to their plate, always with the intention of a brand review, however, I apologised as I recognised this came as a surprise and we should have told them about the assignment and together we should have made the decision on how we would leverage resources to deliver. We agreed moving forward the teams would include all assets in the brief and on the tracker for each campaign and together we would review and assign resources.

Result (including learning)
I followed up with a communication to the team with my direct apology, recognising the situation and how we will adjust the process moving forward.

Analysis
This is a reasonably good example where the candidate admits to their mistake and takes ownership by apologising and working to find a solution going forward.

I would caution against expressing your opinion on a behavioural competency, as tempting as it may be, such as 'I don't believe in mistakes, only opportunities to grow,' which could sound good in a presentation, but in a strict CBI interview, there are no points for expressing opinions and what if you expressed an opinion that the Interviewers didn't agree with, then that could be damaging. There is more likely to be downside than upside.

Your Example for Honest & Integrity
"When have you made a mistake and how did you handle it?'

Context

Actions (what, why, how)

Result

This article on the online publication productmanagerhq.com was shown to me by a client and provides a good insight into what is going on with the 'when have you made a mistake question?' question.

'Hiring managers need to ensure that their organizations become more and more robust and resilient over time. If they bring someone who will crumble under failure, that crumbling will spread like a disease across the organization.

If they bring someone who handles failure with gracefulness, maturity, and wisdom, the organization will most assuredly continue its growth. So, hiring managers want to see that you have the humility to admit mistakes. They want to see whether you have the courage to self-reflect. They want to see whether you have the ability to adapt and course correct. And finally, they want to see how effective you are at drawing lessons from failures, and in applying those to the organization to make the organization antifragile as well'.

Where interviewers are seeking examples for both the Conflict Resolution and the Honesty & Integrity behavioural competencies then it is probably self-evident that strong emotional intelligences (EQ), including low fragility are being sought.

LEADERSHIP

Common CBI questions for Leadership are:
When have you turned around an under-performing team?'
'Tell me about a time when you lead a team that exceeded expectations?'
'Describe a strategic roadmap that you put together to meet a business goal'

Leadership behavioural competency indicators:

- *Develop credibility & trust with your team*
- *Provide the opportunity for your team to develop and grow*
- *Raise the quality of the performance of your team*
- *Develop team moral and spirit*
- *Lead from the front with drive and enthusiasm*
- *See the bigger picture*
- *Delegate well*
- *Be strategic*
- *Comfortable in the detail when required*
- *Build good relationships with other Leaders*
- *Meet or exceed targets*
- *Not afraid of difficult conversations*

You may want to make some notes on your own example before reading examples from others.

Context

Actions (what, why, how)

Result

Example Answer 1 Leadership

Describe a time when you acted as a Servant leader, inspiring the team and enabling talent to succeed?

Context

As Area Sales Manager I recommended a team member be put forward for Area Sales Manager assessment and potential promotion, however, the Senior Leader Team didn't believe his performance merited the assessment for promotion as the sales figures were not strong enough.

Actions

Advised that the team member had come over from a high-performing territory and had moved into a low-performing one that had been on the decline for over 2 years. This team member had been extremely active in building a presence in this market and had revived the sales growth within a short time and that whilst the full turnaround wasn't completely demonstrable in sales figures now it would be within the next 12 months. Argued that the recommendation for assessment was based on performance both for the contribution to sales in the former and new territory.

To support the case for assessment wrote a detailed report, complete with sales graphs and trends.

Result

Analysis and report were accepted, and the individual allowed to go forward to assessment where he passed the assessment, given an Areas Sales Manager secondment, where this individual is performing very well.

Analysis:

There is evidence of servant-leadership here through supporting a team member by putting them forward for promotion, being prepared to have a difficult conversation with the senior leadership team and knowing exactly how much effort the employee had put in, plus being prepared to spend valuable time putting together a detailed report. If the company are awarding points for results, then it helps that the employee proved him correct and he went on to perform well in the role.

Example Answer 2 Leadership

A question often asked of Leaders in an interview is '*When have you turned around an underperforming team?*

Context:
I always ask myself why is somebody underperforming? Nobody likes and aims to under-perform, it doesn't make them feel good. The most challenging area of my business I have had to resource was acoustic tuning

Action
Acoustic tuning is a mixture of science and art, attracting a type of personality that likes the freedom to be creative and often pushes back on processes and disciplines.

Without exception, all the acoustic engineers I have hired have had performance-related areas for improvement. In the case of those who lack discipline, I've tended to pair them with lab technicians who are very process orientated. Thus, catching the creativity and taking away the poor performance in process management. In the case where I have had to manage behaviour performance, I have in some cases provided a more flexible working environment allowing the acoustic engineer to, for example, work at times in the day that better fit with their ability to work creatively.

Result
Invariably this has led to an amicable solution. Providing the end result is excellent and delivered on time I've really accommodated the different cultural requirements of this type of skill set. The key for me is to treat people as individuals understanding what makes them motivated and engaged and providing clear parameters for results at the same time give them the freedom to deliver their best.

Analysis

The candidate talks about improving performance by classing issues into certain groups and whilst I was initially concerned with whether the example would be too general to score, it is sufficiently specific in how the candidate tackles certain types of issues from a senior level. The interviewer should probe deeper to draw out an example where the candidate improved the performance of an individual who themselves did not fall into one of the candidate's previous classifications to gain a deeper appreciation of their ability to turn around a wider set of performance related issues.

Your own example for Leadership:

Tackle questions like *'When have you turned around an under-performing team?' or if your leadership role comes without a dedicated team answer a question such as "Talk about a time when you tried to increase the quality of the performance of people around you?'*

Context

Action (what, why, how)

Result

MANAGING MULTIPLE PRIORITIES

Typically asked with a question like:

'Can you give me an example where you had to manage multiple activities at the same time?'

"When have you had to make tough decisions on what you could accomplish and what couldn't be done in time"

Behavioural competency indicator traits for Managing Multiple Priorities:

- *An ability to differentiate between a range of requests, understanding what is time-critical, what is important and is of lesser importance,*
- *Logical and sound decision-making skills*
- *An ability to plan, but also respond to fluctuating needs and demand*
- *Not afraid to alert stakeholders if there will be a delay*
- *An ability to deliver despite a growing number of demands*
- *An ability to push back if required, but keep stakeholders satisfied*

Notes for your first attempt:

Context

Actions (what, why, how)

Result

Example Answer 1 Managing multiple Priorities (For a Public Sector Organisation)

'When have you had to manage your priorities extremely well?'

Context

I was overseeing a team migrating cases from the current process to the new process. The new process gave us 187 days-notice before a case shutting down on our current system and launching on the new process. Due to an oversight, when choosing the batch of cases to be migrated in December 2016, the CMS (Customer Management System) did not account for the four-day weekend created by Christmas being on a Sunday and treated each day in that period as a regular day. Therefore, on 28th December, we needed to migrate 5 days-worth of cases with limited staff numbers due to people taking holidays.

Action

On sending the "30 days until your case with the current process closes" warning letters on Day 157, we realised the extent of the situation that would occur on December 28th. I immediately made the rest of the team aware, and as changes of circumstances came in for cases still ongoing with the current process, we informed people when they first reported the change that they may encounter a slight delay in their change being processed, I was also able to ask a small group of people to begin preparation work on the cases that would migrate on the 28th, doing account breakdowns early so that on the 28th, we only had to include a couple of weeks extra liability, and maybe one or two extra payments, rather than having to do full breakdowns for all cases on the one day.

I sacrificed the timescales on the ongoing cases over the migration cases - that the cases could not start on the new process until they had all the details, whereas cases still with the current process would continue at their old rate until the new payment schedule was implemented, and children having no support money for a few weeks would be a bigger problem than children having the wrong amount for a few weeks

Result

Although the 28th was still a busy day, by taking everybody off their regular duties, knowing that complaints would be minimised by warning the affected customers in advance, and by doing as much as possible in advance, we were able to get through it, all cases were migrated on time, and by mid-January, we had caught up with the change of circumstance cases as well.

Analysis

Clearly articulates the range of priorities and the actions he is taking to mitigate the issues demonstrating sound decision-making with high quality actions.

Example Answer 2 – Managing Multiple Priorities

From a client on an interview with a global travel firm.

Context

We had overdue payments due to our main Vendor, who worked on 90% of our projects and was currently threatening to walk off all sites with work uncompleted. This would affect our project completion and was a critical risk requiring immediate action above and beyond Business as Usual.

Actions

I needed to diffuse the situation and communicate with Vendor, investigate why we had overdue payments with them, get all the facts, and organise payments urgently due to the risks associated with a large walk-out!

I hastily put together a plan in this order:

1. *Informed Director and contacted the Vendor to arrange a meeting.*
2. *Liaised with Project Managers on overdue payments and find out why the vendor hadn't been paid*
3. *Meet with the vendor, found out their side of the story, listened, negotiated on next steps. Built Relationship/trust.*
4. *Worked with our internal teams, to work on a process for urgent payments to go through and communicated to all.*
5. *Put in place a new process, shared with all, setup monthly meeting with vendor to track project work progress & payments.*
6. *Built better relationship with vendor & PMs,*
7. *Put improved system/process in place,*

8. *Created more regular meetings with all Vendors and PM's*

Result

Resolved issue with Vendor and new structure in place prevented a situation happening again where a vendor/partner would be in the same predicament again.

Analysis

Good in terms of range and quality of actions. Numerically counting the activities emphasises both the number of actions and the order in which the duties were undertaken. The order with which she completes her tasks are demonstrative of the sound decision-making behaviours that you are looking for with this behavioural competency. This could also be used for conflict handling, but with that competency the candidate would want to demonstrate just how bad the conflict was with more detail in how she re-built trust with the vendor.

Your Example for Managing Multiple Priorities

Context

Actions (what, why, how)

Result

PROBLEM-SOLVING

This could be asked with a question such as: '*Can you give me an example of a business issue you resolved?' or 'Tell me about a technical problem you resolved?* Or an interviewer could pick up on something within your CV and ask you to talk them through how you resolved that business problem.

What is Problem Solving all about?

As we saw from the news media story on Elon Musk, with this behavioural competency you want the candidate to walk you through a problem that they resolved, where they had little or no idea of how to resolve the problem in the first place and you want them to talk you through each stage so that you can see their logical and/or lateral thinking all the way through. Any resolution where the candidates knew a considerable amount about the problem in the first place is not an example of problem resolution but of acquired knowledge.

Behavioural competency indicator traits for Problem-Solving:

- *Takes ownership of resolving the business or technical problem*
- *Gets to the root cause of the problem, if possible*
- *Takes a logical approach and work through each step demonstrating what you learned at each step which enabled you to get closer to the resolution*
- *Or take a lateral approach to the problem and demonstrate how this resolved the issue*
- *Achieve a beneficial resolution*

Now that you understand the competency better, what are the potential examples, and which one best demonstrates your logical, lateral, or creative thinking.

Your initial notes for Problem Solving

Context

Actions

Result

Example Answer 1 for Problem Solving

Context

The computer systems had a glitch - the idea was that debt of less than $50 could be written off so as to not cause undue work where the cost of retrieving debt would be larger than the debt itself, however, this caused the system to overlook all loans with repayments of less than $50, regardless of how many payments were missed. I was given a computer report that simply showed all loans that had a debt of over $50, and regular repayments due of less than $50, and was asked to work through it to recover as much debt as possible.

Action

I investigated each case on the list to get a more detailed overview of what had happened. This meant I could divide the list into multiple categories - loans that had never had a repayment, loans where repayments suddenly stopped after a certain date, and loans that had mostly paid continuously but had missed a few payments through the life cycle of the loan. This allowed me to change my approach in the initial contact, depending on what the situation was - in some cases only two payments had been missed and a large amount of the debt was interest. In these scenarios, we agreed to just write off those payments. With loans that had never paid, we agreed to just start over with a clean slate. With loans that clearly had a moment when payments stopped being made, I was able to ask customers what had happened, and if we needed to take hardship into account - if it was just a case of changing bank details but not updating the Direct Debit, we could then arrange a new repayment schedule to incorporate the missing payments.

Result

I was able to contact a majority of the customers on the list and start getting regular payments coming into the bank and I was also able to close off loans that had technically been outstanding for years by writing off a couple of missed payments. I was also able to identify the few cases that did need intervention from debt recovery agents and make sure appropriate action was being taken.

Analysis

A very strong example of applied logic to solve a problem, with a systematic approach to resolving a complex problem. This is also a good example of a candidate who is comfortable with using the pronoun 'I' for all the work he did single-handily, but then uses the pronoun 'We' for when he is working with the other team members. No extra points for that but the interviewers will be grateful.

Example Answer 2 for Problem Solving

This example was delivered to a global business for a Marketing Director role, originally for Customer Service, but as you will see it is an even better example of Problem Solving.

Context

Following careful expert review, a difficult decision was made to pause further patient recruitment into a clinical study. This decision would be devastating to the patients as this was their hope for a treatment.

Action

Facing a situation where our decision needed to be made via a press release there was a chance that the patient community would first read the news in the media, so I developed the press release and associated collateral and also rapidly convened and led a matrix team to develop a communications cascade plan that covered multiple stakeholders including patients, patients' groups, regulators and suppliers.

I was conscious that the study results were hugely disappointing to the team, and we all knew this would be devasting news to the patients. It was highly emotional with media speculation. I did not want the team to get distracted by the media so took the lead to convene a cross-matrix team. In doing so, the team was aligned with each individual clear on the comms required to their respective stakeholder group as soon as the press release was issued. The communication cascade was implemented like clockwork and, most importantly, we were able to connect with the patients/patient groups, so they were informed ahead or soon after the media.

In addition, aligned with our focus on patients, I developed a group mailbox to triage the expected patient enquiries.

Result:

The process that I put in place was shared with another team in readiness for their project that was potentially facing a similar situation. Key learning would have been to have this in place for any project where there is an active patient community.

Analysis

This example demonstrates that the candidate has a firm grasp on all the conflicting needs of the business, the reporting commitments, the organisation reputation and has built a solution that addresses all of these aspects. The candidate is also aware of the real impact on the patients, though for customer service example would want to add more actions related to customer focus with less problem-solving actions, other than the ones that cross-over into indicators for customer service, for example connecting with patients/patient groups, so they were informed ahead or soon after the media.

Your example for Problem Solving

When have you resolved a problem for your business where you had little or no knowledge of how to resolve the problem initially?

Context

Action (what, why, how)

Result

INFLUENCE & PERSUASION

Common CBI questions include:

'What would be a good example of your influences and persuasion skills?' or

'When have you managed to win an account because of your influence and persuasion skills?'

Behavioural competency indicator traits for Influence & Persuasion:

- *Listening and understanding the needs of others*
- *Ability to communicate at the right level according to your audience*
- *Ability to articulate the benefits of what you are proposing that are of interest to your audience*
- *Understand the strengths and weaknesses of your own position and that of those you are attempting to persuade*
- *Ability to appreciate and handle objections*
- *Identify advocates who will support your position*

Notes for your own example

Context

Actions (what, why, how)

Results

Example Answer 1 for Influence & Persuasion

Context

A project that I was working on had a primary objective to upgrade a system that was reaching the end of its supported life. As a business analyst, I was asked to look for other business opportunities that could be incorporated without threatening the timeline or driving up budget costs.

Action

After positioning this with stakeholders, users from a number of business areas were very passionate about describing potential benefits to them that could be included. I received far more requirements than could be accommodated by the delivery

This was solved by communication and logic. The logic was achieved by reviewing each of the requirements against a 'so what' set of criteria as to the tangible benefits that would be gained in terms of costs and time saved versus the extent to which the change could be incorporated alongside the change being made without introducing significant time, cost or additional risk to the immovable deadline

From a communication perspective, the headline constraint of only being able to fit in requirements around the areas being configured had already been shared, however using this indisputable logic allowed all stakeholders to be able to see how their requests stacked up against other options and why ultimately, they were included or not

Results

A number of achievable 'wins' were incorporated alongside the system upgrade which drove efficiency for the business. Stakeholders felt engaged and bought into the process and there was clear sight around the prioritisation logic

Analysis

This is an above-average example for both Problem Solving and Influence and Persuasion, but it is worth understanding that before you start you are clear on which behavioural competency you are answering with your example, rather than attempt to do both at the same time. If it is Problem Solving then focus more on the problem and the steps you took to the resolution and if it is Persuasion and Influence, then go into more detail on the traits associated with that behavioural competency.

Example Answer 2 for Influence & Persuasion

Context

I put forward the idea of a Competency-Based Interview workshop to an outplacement company, not long after starting with them and noting that whilst they had interview workshops, they didn't have a specific workshop on CBI.

Action

I put it to the Operations Director, making the case for why we should have a CBI workshop and the potential demand there would be from our clients and although she expressed a definite interest at the time, there were no signals in the following weeks that this would be happening anytime soon. I realised that I needed another approach, that either I hadn't made the case well enough or that the logic and reasoning given weren't enough on their own.

I had noticed in the time that I had been there, that she tended to listen to certain senior coaches that had been there longer. I approached one of these coaches and put the idea to her, she was immediately favourable and was able to inform me on what the Operations Director would want to know before going ahead with such a suggestion, such as utilising pre-agreed templates for workshops and using common internal language. She was aware that some CBI workshops had been done off-site before and that by incorporating some of these workshop presentation slides it would be an easier sell to the Operations Director. We would not be 're-inventing the wheel'.

This Coach found the pre-existing slides and I utilised what I could from these to develop our own slides and materials and although the workshop looked cosmetically similar, the content was far richer, and the exercises were better designed to develop CBI skills for the participants. The senior coach organised a subsequent meeting for us with the Operations Director and in this meeting, we both emphasised the continuation of what had gone before, the pre-agreed templates and documentation, and constructed this presentation with more internal language.

Result

We got the go-ahead to roll out the workshop. As soon as it was launched it became one of the most popular workshops on offer and we went from one workshop every 2 weeks to 2 a week with very high satisfaction rates. This also became the standard workshop on CBI should we or any other coach be asked to deliver it off-site.

Analysis:

You rarely hear a straight no in business, so understanding how to react, build up your advocates, understand what the objections could be, and then build your case to negate the objections as well as promote the positives. Perhaps doing all of the above before going to their Operations Director in the first time would have been even smarter, but I believe there is good evidence of quality and content for Persuasion & Influence.

Your Own Example for Influence & Persuasion

Context

Actions (what, why, how)

Results

CHALLENGING ACCEPTED PRACTICES

Which could be asked in questions such as:
'When have you challenged the status quo?'
'Tell me about a time when you did the right things?'

This behavioural competency is often sought within organisations where continuous innovation and change are the normal practice, but there is often a surge in its popularity across sectors especially when there has been a scandal, such as within the Investment Banking sector during the Banking crisis and within Financial Services after the PPI scandal.

Key behavioural competency indicators for challenging the status quo:

- *Can appreciate the reasoning for both the current method and for the new approach*
- *Strength of conviction to challenge*
- *Builds good evidence for change, understanding any potential risk for change*
- *Appreciate that there is likely to be resistance to change and is adept at handling the resistance*
- *Perseverance*
- *Resilience*

Notes for your own example:

Context

Action (what, why, how)

Result

Example Answer 1 to Challenging Accepted Practices

This was the response to the question 'When have you challenged the status quo?'

Context

This is from when I was a technical infrastructure lead with responsibility for telephony solutions, at a financial institution. A Chief Executive level decision was made for a major investment rather than piecemeal upgrades to the technology infrastructure. This was a major decision that we had sought for many years. A task force was assembled consisting of infrastructure leads of which I was one, plus other stakeholders such as finance, who were tasked with planning this initiative.

Actions

On reviewing The Board's strategic direction, I noted that it included that all locations were to have the same features and functions, operational costs to be reduced, with business initiatives unconstrained by technology limitations. It took many months to finalise a recommendation and we split the process into logical subsections. There were multiple telephony solutions co-existing at that time, and new locations were equipped with a standard solution agreed upon some years earlier. At one meeting the draft recommendation stated that the current telephony solution would be used. This was my area, so I said that I assumed this was simply a placeholder since it had not been debated. The general response to my question was that we had a working solution, it was assumed my opinion was to continue as is, why would we change it. I asked that we reconvene over the next few days to deliberate this matter. My view was that I was open to alternatives, and as a group, we needed to either properly ratify the status quo or recommend an alternative. In one-to-one and group meetings I explained the market and technology had shifted since adopting the current solution, we had to live with this decision for probably 8-10 years, therefore it was worth a few weeks of exploration.

Result

As a result, we investigated options and implemented a more radical solution providing greater business flexibility and a consistent global solution.

Analysis

Clear evidence of challenging assumptions made on her behalf and strength in her own conviction by taking a different view to the one held by the group, which proved to be a better decision for the long term.

Example 2 Challenging Accepted Practices

When did you do the right thing?

Context *Many of the products under my responsibility involves liaison with partners where milestones/decisions were often considered financially material to them or critical to stakeholder value.*

Action *For one such partner, we worked very closely to agree on language pertaining to a project. My review team was US-based and having arrived at work one morning, read an email informing that they (the partner) planned to issue a press release within the next hour. I did not agree with the conclusion of the press release, nor did I think that it was right that the partner gave limited time to review. In the absence of my review team, I took full accountability to try to pause their press release by sending an email, requesting an urgent call to discuss my concerns, and escalating to senior leadership.*

I balanced the risk of causing an issue with our partners without input from the broader team versus the consequences of having information in the public domain without review by our signatories. Given that the news could be reported in the media, as well as informing the project team, I also did not want it to come as a surprise to senior leadership.

Result & Learning *The partner issued the press release, but all internal stakeholders were informed ahead so they were aware that attempts had been made to pause plans. While the partner press release was still issued, my communication provided documented evidence that my company did not approve of the approach. This supported a senior leader's email to the partner that their actions did not reflect the collaborative behaviour that we expected from our partners.*

Analysis Often what can hold people back from doing the right thing is a lack of confidence in endangering an important relationship with an important stakeholder. Here the candidate takes decisive action and escalates it to the highest level. Not all situations require this level of action but given the nature of the action by the partner then this candidate's action seems the most appropriate one. Good level of range and quality of actions pertaining to doing the right thing/challenging accepted practices.

Your own example for challenging accepted practices

Context

Action (what, why, how)

Result

DEALING WITH AMBIGUITY

Common questions

'Tell me about a time when you had to deliver a project with an ambiguous roadmap'

'When have you had to deal with a significant amount of ambiguity in your role?'

Indicators for the Behaviour traits associated with dealing with ambiguity;

- *Take ownership, even when the path is unclear*
- *Resourceful, can find a way, play to your strengths*
- *Agility in planning and activity*
- *Comfortable in reaching out and talking to others more knowledgeable*
- *Have faith in yourself*
- *Objective self-analysis of progress and willing to change if necessary*

Notes for your own example

Context

Action

Result

Example Answer 1 Dealing with Ambiguity

Context *Brand X (name removed to protect anonymity) had a rudimentary stamp card loyalty system which rewarded high spenders with cash vouchers and wanted a more sophisticated card loyalty programme.*

Action *On Product Management:*
Started a project brief with our CRM agency to use segmentation data to develop an online portal.

Created a product roadmap with milestones for use with the agency to ensure key features were built well and were on-brand.
On Operations:
Collaborated with retail team to ensure operations of in-store redemptions and service delivery was streamlined.
Marketing/brand: Assessed the SWOT in terms of customer impact when changing the program. Realised a need to build perceived value of the program's rewards. Started a countdown campaign focused on the loyalty gifts' exclusivity.
Created arbitrage issues where customers bought in bulk and resold online or in China. Addressed impact on brand image.
Built a new online loyalty system in Q1, with digital tracking of points and redemption where rewards were items & services, not vouchers.
close follow-up ensured that the project stayed on schedule. Delivered in a quarter.
Result *During launch week the buzz around the launch resulted in around YYYY shares/engagement, we topped social listening ranks for beauty brands in Singapore. Singapore team was the first to revamp its CRM system. 1st time as leader of best practices - we were a case study for other countries to follow on adopting the CRM revamp.*

Analysis The candidate has described many actions that are indicators of the required behavioural competencies as it pertains to taking ownership, being resourceful, agile, collaborating and having faith in themselves.

Example Answer 2 Dealing with Ambiguity

Context *Of all the examples that I could choose I kept coming back to the most recent one. The context of which was that I thought it was the right time to write a book on CBI.*

Action *Although I felt confident in my knowledge on the subject and had coached CBI skills for more than 8 years, apart from pulling together some presentation material for a workshop which was done in partnership with a colleague, I had no previous experience of writing a book, let alone publishing one as well.*

Whilst starting on the content of the book, I built up a picture of the unknowns, such as how formal or informal should the narrative be? What content would be of most interest to a reader? What would be the right look and feel of the book? was it better to work with a publisher or publish myself? Whilst writing, I maintained research with clients to keep-up-to date on CBI questions being asked and felt that a significant section with examples in would be most helpful for readers to know what they should be looking to produce themselves.

As the content started coming together and as my writing and editing started to improve a little, I began to tackle some more of the unknowns. I tested the concept with some of my clients, some of whom were not only supportive, but also gave me their own understanding of what they would want from such a publication. I reached out to people I knew that work or did work for publishing companies and sought their advice. I sent in a draft to a Publishing House that I thought would be the one most likely to be interested in this genre and whilst I'm still waiting to hear, the process of articulating the concept and sending in example chapters further helped in the development of the book. I felt more confident that I could write and publish the book without a publisher and started to watch plenty of online tutorials on self-publishing. All the time setting aside sufficient hours per week to keep writing and improving the content.

Result *If you are reading this book and it has been helpful for you then that is a significant outcome. Sales will only come if the product is good enough.*

Analysis

I believe this example meets the indicators of the key behavioural traits for this competency, some of them to a high degree, others to a lesser extent.

Your own example for dealing with Ambiguity

Context

Actions

Result

ADDITIONAL QUESTIONS & ANSWERS

Throughout my time delivering CBI workshops and 1 to 1 session a number of common questions come up far more often than others from clients who are just getting to grips with putting together their own examples, some of which could also be occurring to you now, as you put more of your own examples together, so I have tried to answer them here.

Can I use the same example for different behavioural competencies?

Whilst it would be ideal to be able to utilise different events each time, some events in our careers/experiences draw greater on our behavioural competencies and might provide far richer examples than other events. In this scenario, when drawing on the same event, whilst there would be similarity potentially in the Context, the Actions and Results would be somewhat different as you would be focusing on the Actions that you took that are relevant for each respective behavioural competency and the Result as it pertained to each behavioural competency should also be different.

How far can I go back in time?

In theory, you can go back as far as you like, the principle being that if you have demonstrated that level of behaviour competency once before, then you can do it again. But in reality, if you are continuously using examples drawn from a long time ago, then that would likely be of concern to the interviewers, who would probably ask you for some examples which happened more recently.

Can the example be an event that didn't occur at work?

Yes, the principle being that it is a behavioural competency and that if you can demonstrate it at the level required outside of work then you can do it just as well inside. Again, in reality I would recommend that the vast majority of examples come from a work-based environment, unless of course you are a recent graduate or have recently left college or school.

Can I attempt to demonstrate more than one behavioural competency in an example answer?

I would advise against this as I tend to find that when candidates try to do this, they haven't succeeded in demonstrating enough range and/or quality of actions that meet an acceptable level of the behavioural competency that was being asked for in the question.

Will I be told if the interview will be a CBI?

Best practice dictates that the company inform all candidates ahead of the interview that they will be receiving a CBI and give each candidate equal notice. Many companies adhere to this practice, whilst other companies will mix in CBI questions with non-CBI questions and in this scenario, they are less likely to provide prior notice.

ADDITIONAL WORKBOOK

For attempting more CBI answers

Context

Actions (what, why, how)

Result

Context

Actions (what, why, how)

Results

Context

Actions (what, why, how)

Results

Context

Actions (what, why, how)

Results

Context

Actions (what, why, how)

Results

Context

Actions (what, why, how)

Results

Context

Actions (what, why, how)

Results

Printed in Great Britain
by Amazon

78035897R00072